A **SporTellers**™ Book

PLAY-OFF

BENJAMIN SWIFT

A Pacemaker® Program

Fearon Education
a division of
David S. Lake Publishers
Belmont, California

F
SWI

SporTellers™

Senior development editor: Christopher Ransom Miller
Content editor: Carol B. Whiteley
Production editor: Mary McClellan
Design manager: Eleanor Mennick
Illustrator: Bob Haydock
Cover: Bob Haydock

ISBN–0–8224–6480–2
Library of Congress Catalog Card Number: 80–82987
Printed in the United States of America.
1.9 8 7 6 5 4

Contents

CHAPTER 1

On Their Way

It was Rick's first year as a professional running back. He played for the Philadelphia Eagles, and he was good. After he had played only four games, sportswriters in many places started calling him the brightest running star of the season. With his help, his team had won every game so far. Many people believed the Eagles would win their division title. That would put them in one of the play-offs leading to the Super Bowl.

The Eagles were playing today. But Rick wasn't with them. He had hurt his leg in the game the week before, and it still wasn't better. The team's doctor had told him to stay home today so that he would be ready to play in the big game against Houston next week.

Now Rick sat at home watching television. The game Rick was watching wasn't the one the Eagles were playing. That game wasn't being televised. As Rick sat with his leg resting on a soft chair, he watched two teams from another division fighting for first place. Rick studied them well. The team that won might be in the same play-off as the Eagles. If both Philadelphia and Minnesota won their division titles, they would play against each other for the right to play in the Super Bowl.

Rick watched the picture on the television as it showed one player over and over again. The man's name was Mike Huggard, and he played for the Vikings. He was the best defensive linebacker in the league. He took his place, waiting for the other team to move the ball.

The camera went in close again, showing a giant of a man. Huggard's arms and legs looked strong, and his face had a hard, tough look. One sportswriter in Minneapolis had named him Mountain Man.

Rick's hands closed and opened as he watched the play start. A Packer running back took the ball and ran toward the line. A hole opened up. The back went into it. He started to move through. But Mike Huggard was waiting for him. Huggard hit the man hard.

Rick could almost feel it. He shook his head. Huggard was good. He watched as the man stood up and moved back to his own side. The runner he had tackled took his time getting up from the ground.

One of the television announcers was talking about the Mountain Man as the two teams faced off again.

It's a big day for Mountain Man. We all knew Mike Huggard was going to be a real pro when he left college. You don't make All-American for nothing. But every year this linebacker gets better.

The other announcer broke in.

That's right, Leon. At 270 pounds, Huggard is a Mountain Man, all right. I'm glad I'm not playing running back against him.

The game went on. Mike Huggard's team widened its lead. And Huggard kept playing a really great game. He was knocking down the other team's quarterback every time he could. He stopped the running backs too, with hard, clean tackles.

Soon the last play of the game was starting. The Packers were about to lose the game. Their quarterback dropped back to pass. As the Green Bay player looked for his receiver, Mike Huggard came rocketing through the line. He hit the quarterback before the ball could leave his hand.

Mountain Man.

The two announcers had spoken at the same time.

"Mountain Man," Rick said as he turned off the television. If things went the way he thought they would, one day soon he would be running against Mountain Man Huggard. He didn't like the idea. He did like the idea of his own team winning its division title, of being in the play-offs, of going to the Super Bowl. But he didn't want to play against big Mike Huggard in any game.

Because Mike was tough.

Because Mike was hard on running backs.

Because Mike was Rick's older brother.

CHAPTER 2
Inside Mountain Man

Up in Minnesota, Mike Huggard was washing the dirt of the playing field off his body. The water felt good as it poured down and spilled over him. Mike had played hard, as he did in every game. And he hurt all over, as he did after every game.

Other players stood next to Mike, talking to one another about the game. No one spoke much to Mike. But it was always that way. The men liked having him on the Vikings team, and Mike knew that. He was a great player. But he wasn't someone most people could talk to in an easy way. The other players weren't afraid of Mike. But they left him by himself a lot of the time.

Mike turned off the water and walked into the locker room to dress. He pulled out his street clothes and sat down on a bench next to Dan Becker. Dan was a defensive tackle. He was almost as large as Mike but not as fast a runner. Dan did his job well, and everyone on the team liked him. It was as easy for Dan to make friends as it was to play football. He was Mike Huggard's only real friend on the Vikings.

"Good game you played today," Dan said as he put on his shoes. He had already dressed and was just about to leave for home.

Mike nodded as he pulled on his light blue shirt. "You too, Dan," he said.

"I wasn't bad," Dan joked. "But you were out to kill them."

Mike lifted his head up with a start and looked hard at Dan. "I'm never out to kill anyone."

"You know what I mean, Mike," Dan said. "You just gave it that much more. The way you always do."

"They pay me to play. I try to earn my money," Mike said in a quiet voice.

"Can I write that in the newspaper, Mike?"

Mike looked behind him. The voice came from Pamela Gray, a reporter. She was walking toward Mike through the rows of laughing players and dirty uniforms. "Can I put that down?" she asked. "You just try to earn your money?"

Mike smiled. "Why not? I'm a pro," he said. "I play for money."

"You have to play for more than that. Everyone in pro football plays for money," Gray said. "But they don't all play the way you do, Mike."

Mike was dressed now and ready to go. He didn't answer the reporter. He closed the door to his locker and was about to leave.

"I'd really like to talk to you and find out more about you, Mike. No one has ever written a really good story about the Mountain Man," Gray told him. "I'd like to try. How about it?"

Mike shook his head. He started to turn toward the door.

"Wait, Mike," Gray said. "Can't we—?"

"No," Dan Becker said to her.

Gray looked at Mike and then at Dan. "Thanks a lot," she said in a voice that didn't mean it. Then she went to talk to some other players.

"You don't have to take care of me, Dan," Mike Huggard said as the reporter walked away.

"No one knows that better than I do, Mike. I just knew you didn't want to talk to her any longer," Dan told him.

"You were right," Mike said. He stood next to the bench, but his mind was far away.

"Is something troubling you, Mike?"

Mike looked at his friend. "Did I say that?"

"You know you didn't. But you seem a little on edge," Dan told him.

Mike shook his head. "I'm fine."

"I hope so," Dan said. "But if you're not, here's something that should make you happy. After today, we're looking good for our division title."

"I know," Mike said in a soft voice.

"Doesn't that make you happy, Mike?"

Mike turned. "Maybe not," he said. With a wave to Dan, he headed for the door. But on the way, he heard someone talking about him. It was one of the other players talking to Pamela Gray.

Mike kept walking when he heard what the other man said: "It's just that I think Mike Huggard's got ice in his blood."

* * *

Mike left the playing field and started walking toward his small home near the stadium. The leaves on the trees were red and yellow. The air was cool. There was a light wind. Winter would be coming soon. People had on warm coats and rushed along the streets to keep warm.

Mike liked the city well enough. It was his home for the football season. But he liked the small town where he and his brother Rick had grown up even better. He hadn't lived there for some time, though.

Six years ago, when Mike had finished high school, he had gone on to college in another part of the state. Two years after that, Rick had left home too. Rick had gone on to a different college. The days when the two happy brothers had been home together seemed very long ago.

It had been fun growing up together. Mike and Rick had been close. They had had a few fights, of course. But for the most part, they had enjoyed being together. Mike was really pleased when it turned out that Rick loved football too.

As kids, the two brothers had played the game often—just for fun. They played hard and to win. But they tried not to hurt each other. Their father, a preacher, had always told them to love each other—on the football field and off.

Mike remembered a talk he and Rick had had with their quiet, strong father a long time ago. It was soon after their mother had died, so everything their father said and did mattered a lot to the two boys. Mr. Huggard had called them over after he watched them play a hard game of tackle ball.

"You're brothers, you two," he had said. "You must always remember that. Brothers love each other. And they never try to hurt each other. You don't want to hurt Rick, do you, Mike?"

"No, Pop," Mike had answered.

"And you, Rick?"

"I don't want to hurt Mike either," Rick had told his father.

"In football, you can hurt a player you're playing against," Mr. Huggard had explained.

"So you never want to play hard against each other. But you can play hard against other teams. You'll be on the same team next year in school. Give it everything you've got. Play to win, because that's what the team will want you to do. And what you'll want to do too. But when you play against each other, remember who you are. You're brothers."

Mike had always remembered that talk, and it had changed him. After that talk, he had always tried to help Rick—to work with him on plays when Rick had made the high school team and to teach him everything he knew. Rick looked up to his big, strong brother and was his best fan. The two boys found out that their father was right. They loved each other, though they never said it out loud.

For the two years that Mike and Rick had played high school football together, their team was the best their town had ever had. Both boys had been wanted by many colleges. It had been a great time. But then Mike had gone his way. And soon Rick had gone his.

Mike found himself smiling as he walked along remembering the old days. But the smile left his face as he remembered where he

was—and where Rick was. His little brother
was a pro now too, on another team and in
another division. There was no more helping
each other out or teaching each other tricks of
the trade. Times had changed. Things were
different now. Mike and Rick might find
themselves face to face on the playing field—
something Mike had been worrying about
since Rick decided to turn pro.

Suddenly, Mike saw a small cat walking
slowly across the street. A large truck was
coming right at it. A young child stood at the
side of the street. She was pointing at the cat
and crying.

Mike ran. He ran as fast as he did on the football field. He got to the cat, just before the truck did, and picked it up. As he jumped out of the way, he heard the big truck wheels screaming to a stop. But the cat was safe, and Mike waved the truck on.

Turning toward the child, Mike held up the cat to show her it was OK. Then he took it and put it in the little girl's arms. She smiled through her tears. Mike smiled back. Then he turned to leave.

As he stepped forward, a man's voice called out to him, "Thank you!"

Mike turned to find a man running down the street. "You saved Ellen's cat," the man said to Mike as he reached the place where Mike and the little girl stood. Then he picked up the child, who still had the cat in her arms. "I'm Larry Johnson," the man told Mike. "Thank you again."

"I'm glad I was around at the right time," Mike said.

"You could have been hurt," Mr. Johnson said. "I saw it from the living room window. I was sure that the truck would hit Muffin. But you were fast. I've never seen a man as big as you move that fast!"

Mike smiled. "I didn't want your girl to lose her cat."

"You put your life on the line to make sure that didn't happen. Not many would, Mr.—? Wait a minute," Mr. Johnson said. "I know you, don't I?"

"I walk down this street a lot," Mike said.

"I don't mean from around here. I mean on television. You're a football player. You're Mike Huggard!"

Mike nodded. People were always coming up to him on the street and telling him that they knew who he was. Mike knew that he had become famous to a lot of people. But it had never made him feel easy. Being famous was not why he played football. He played it because that was what he could do best. And he always liked to do his best.

"Yes, I'm Mike Huggard," Mike said in a soft voice.

"Well, you're a great football player," Mr. Johnson said.

"Thank you," Mike said. It was all he could think of to say. He didn't enjoy it when people made a big thing about who he was. As he watched the little girl holding her cat, he was glad she would think of him only as someone who had been nice to her, not as a famous football player.

"You know something, though," Mr. Johnson went on. "I just didn't think that someone like you. . . ."

Mike looked at the man. "Yes?"

"Well, you were so nice just now. But you seem so different when I watch you play football. Hard. And. . . ."

Mike stopped him. "Mean?"

"I'm sorry, Mr. Huggard. I didn't mean anything. I just. . . ."

"It's all right," Mike said. "A lot of people think about me that way. But I'm just doing my job out on the field. Doing my best, and trying to win."

"I understand," Mr. Johnson said. "But I'm glad to find out about the softer side of you too. I'm really happy to have met you."

Mike smiled again. "I'm happy to have met you too." Then he looked at the little girl. "Keep hold of that cat now," he said. And then he was on his way.

Mike felt good as he walked down the street. It was nice to meet a caring family. But talking to the little girl and her father made him think about Rick once more. He had read that his brother had been hurt in the game against the Chargers the week before. He had been wanting to call him all week—to see how he was and to see if he would be playing again soon. Talking to Larry Johnson made Mike want to call Rick even more.

Then Mike shook his head. He couldn't call Rick. He had been worrying all season that this year he and Rick would meet in the play-offs. Now it looked as if they would. And talking to Rick would only remind Mike of how much he didn't want to be in that play-off game.

CHAPTER 3

Down and Out

The following week, winter came to Philadelphia. A light snow fell as the Eagles dressed for their first night game. The game was against the Chicago Bears, and it was being televised on Monday Night Football. The Eagles were leading their division, and winning every game was important.

The game started with a bang. The Eagles ran back the opening kick for a touchdown. But the Bears soon tied things up.

Rick couldn't seem to get his running game started. In fact, he wasn't playing well at all. Up in the announcer's box, Howard Cosell talked about Rick's poor game:

I believe I know why Rick Huggard is playing so badly tonight. In the games before this one, no one knew what he would do. He was new to professional football, and it was anyone's guess how he would play.

Now he's got several games behind him. Games in which he was good—very good. But tonight he's up against a team that has given him a real studying. The Bears have watched movies of Rick Huggard running against other teams. And they have his number. They are showing that. Because they are stopping him again and again.

Rick is new to the kinds of tests pro players must go through. But there is another reason why I think Rick Huggard is looking so bad. He has played in enough games now to know that professional football can be ugly and dirty.

And I think that frightens him. Rick Huggard has learned he can get hurt. He has been hurt on the playing field. He knows he can be hurt again. So he is playing against men who have his number. And he is playing frightened.

I'm sorry that Rick Huggard is having so much trouble in this tough game. It's a hard life. But right this minute I'm sure I'm not as sorry as his coaches or his teammates.

Down on the field, Rick was feeling a lot of heat, even though the weather was cold. His offensive unit had the ball. It was third down and two. The Eagles were in a huddle.

The quarterback, Johnny Wolfe, looked at Rick. Rick knew that Wolfe was making up his mind about calling a play for Rick. The quarterback kept watching him. Then he said, "You want the ball, Rick?"

"Sure," Rick answered. But for the first time in his football life, he wasn't sure he could handle the ball. He wasn't playing well. And he didn't know why.

Wolfe called a play that Rick had used to make a lot of yards in the past. It was a play in which the quarterback looked as if he were going to pass. But as he moved back, he would hand off the ball to Rick. The defensive linemen for the other team would be drawn toward the quarterback. But Rick would be running around the left end—with the ball.

The Eagles broke from the huddle and took their places. Rick rubbed his hands on his knees. Then Wolfe called the play and took the ball from the center. He moved back, and Rick ran to the side. Then Rick ran close to

Wolfe, taking the ball from the quarterback's hands.

Holding the ball close, Rick moved out toward the left end of the line. He always loved this kind of run, turning on the speed and escaping from the line of players set on pulling him down. But now his legs seemed heavy. He couldn't find his speed. He was hit a yard short of a first down. He went down hard under the big body of a Bears tackle.

Rick got up and left the field, his head down. His team would have to kick. He hadn't pulled off the play.

When he reached the bench, he sat by himself on the far side. He didn't want to talk to anyone. And he didn't want to watch the play on the field.

Minutes later, the coach came over and sat down beside him. He looked at Rick, who sat looking at the ground. When the coach spoke, his voice was kind. "What seems to be wrong, Rick?"

Rick shook his head. He didn't answer because he didn't know what was wrong.

"I saw you rub your leg before," the coach said. "Is it hurting you?"

"No," Rick answered.

"You feel all right then?"

"Yes."

The coach didn't say anything more for a short time. Then he said, "I'll give you a rest, Rick. Maybe that's the best thing to do." He got up and headed back to the edge of the field.

After the Bears missed a first down, they had to give up the ball. When the kick took place, Rick should have been on the field playing again. But the coach left him on the bench. Another man was sent in to play in his place.

As Rick sat thinking about his problem, he wondered if his brother Mike was watching the game on television. If he was, he wouldn't like the way Rick had been playing. He had never liked it when Rick hadn't played well without a reason. Mike had always played well. Rick had even asked him about it once. And he still remembered Mike's answer.

Mike had said, "If you're going to do something, you better do it hard and well. Or why do it at all?"

Mike had made it seem so simple. And after hearing Mike's words, Rick had always played as hard as he could. But had he been doing that tonight? Rick knew that he hadn't.

Suddenly, after thinking about his brother, Rick knew why. He knew why he had been playing so badly against the Bears. It was because he didn't want to play against Mike in a play-off game.

And if Rick's team lost the game that night, and then a few others later, they wouldn't be in any play-off.

Rick finally knew that that was the reason. He wasn't playing well so he could keep from meeting his brother on the field. But as he sat on the cold wood bench, he knew he was letting down his coaches, his trainer, his teammates. Everyone.

Howard Cosell looked down at Rick as the Eagles' second string player went in for him. In that familiar voice, Cosell spoke.

I can see that young Rick Huggard is being kept on the bench. It's a smart move. Because tonight we have seen without question that Rick Huggard is not the football player he was talked up to be. He is not the player that his great linebacker brother Mike is. I'm sorry Rick is having his problems. I've talked to that nice young man more than once. I like him. And I'm sorry to see that he is not working out.

CHAPTER 4

The Reason Why

Far from the Eagles' playing field, two men sat watching television. One of the men was Dan Becker, tackle for the Minnesota Vikings. The other was Dan's friend and teammate, Mike Huggard. As the football game moved forward, Mike's eyes took on a dark look.

A few minutes before the half, Dan Becker spoke. "Is Cosell right? About Rick not being the football player you are?"

"No," said Mike. "He's as good as I am. But we play different positions. I'm a linebacker. Rick is a runner. A good runner."

"Not tonight, Mike," Dan said.

Mike didn't answer. He just sat in his chair without moving.

Soon the last play of the first half was over. The TV camera showed crowded stands and then the playing field. Rick Huggard could be seen slowly heading for the locker room.

"Looks like Rick is out of it for this game," Dan Becker said to his friend beside him. "Do you think his leg is giving him trouble?"

"I don't know."

Dan waited, but Mike didn't go on. "Do you think Rick is afraid? Because he got hurt so early in the season?"

"I don't know that either," Mike said. "I haven't talked to him. But I don't think so. He was never afraid before."

Dan looked hard at his friend. "But he never played pro ball before."

Mike looked back at Dan. "Getting hurt is part of the game, Dan. Rick knew that before he started. He knew that he might not play long. And he knew that he would have to give up playing if he got hurt badly. So did you. So did I."

Dan moved his large body around on the soft pillow on which he lay. "So why do we do it? Why do we put our bodies on the line all season?"

"The money," Mike answered.

"You always say that, Mike. And it's true for some of the players. But it's got to be more than that for most of us. Tell me the real story. Why do you play a game in which at any minute you can be broken in two?"

Mike said nothing for a while. Then he took a deep breath. "I play football because it's the thing I do best. I'll play as long as I think I can play well. As long as I can help the team. Then, when the time comes. . . ."

Dan dropped his head. No football player liked to think about leaving the game. He said, "Yes?"

"When the time comes for me to stop playing, I'll do something different. I've put my mind and body into football. I'll put them into something else later, and I'll do it just as well."

"Such as?"

"I don't know yet, Dan. I'll find that out when I need to."

Neither man spoke again for a while. But as the second half of the game was about to start, Dan asked one more question. "Do you ever think about playing against your brother? It can happen if we both win our divisions."

Mike took another deep breath and let it out slowly. "I think about it all the time. I haven't told anyone else. But since the beginning of the season, I've thought of nothing else. I don't think I'll have to worry about it after tonight, though. The way the Eagles are playing in this game, they'll lose it for sure."

"But if you *did* have to play against Rick, you could stop him easy."

"That's your guess," Mike said.

"You could stop him easy tonight, that's for sure," Dan said. "What *is* the matter with him, Mike?"

Mike's eyes grew dark again. He folded his arms across his chest as he watched the Eagles run out on the field for the start of the second half. When he didn't speak, Dan said, "Mike?"

"He isn't trying," Mike finally said. His voice was angry.

"But why not? This game is important to them."

Mike didn't answer. He thought he knew why Rick wasn't trying very hard. But he didn't want to talk about it.

"Maybe he'll pick up in this half," Dan said.

Again, Mike didn't answer.

CHAPTER 5

Back in the Game

Rick started the second half of the game against the Bears sitting on the bench again. He had said nothing during the coach's talk in the locker room. The coach had asked everyone to play harder, to keep on their toes more. But Rick hadn't really listened. He had been thinking. He had been trying to decide what it was he had to do.

At last he had found the answer. But he was not sure that he was ready to act on it. Or that he *could* act on it.

Now he listened to another player who sat on the bench beside him. "We've got to get going," the player said. "If we drop this game, it's a tie for the lead. If we drop the next one, we might fall out of first place. Too many bad games, no play-off. No Super Bowl. If. . . ."

The coach, who stood on the edge of the field, turned around and cut the player off. "We play one game at a time on this team. And that one game is against the Bears. Now, I want everyone to forget everything but this one game."

The player stopped talking, but Rick kept thinking. Yes, he thought. One game at a time. Mike had always said that too. If you worry too much about what might be up front, you can play a bad game. You should think about only what is happening right now.

Rick stood up. He walked over to the coach. "I want in," he said. He felt strong.

The coach looked at him for what seemed like a long time. Finally he said, "Go in, then. At the end of this play."

In seconds, Rick was out on the field. He met the rest of the team in the huddle. But they weren't sure they were happy to have him there. Everyone knew that Rick's game was off. They didn't know how well Rick could run now.

Rick knew by the other men's looks that they were worried about what he would do. He would have to show them he was back in

one piece. But Johnny Wolfe, the quarterback, didn't let Rick run the next play. It was
a pass play. Rick would have to block.

Rick looked at the big men on the Bears'
team getting ready to move. He set himself.
He listened to Wolfe call the play. Then Wolfe
took the ball from the center and dropped
back. Rick rushed toward his man, who was
after the receiver. With a strong block, Rick
knocked the man to the ground, leaving the
receiver wide open. The receiver caught the
ball and made 16 yards.

On the way to the huddle, Johnny Wolfe
caught up with Rick. "Nice block, Rick," he
said. "It made that play work."

"Thanks," Rick said. He had learned how to
block from his brother Mike. Mike had also
taught him how to kick, tackle, and pass. But
now he hoped he would be asked to take the
ball and run with it. The Eagles' quarterback
looked as if he were thinking about it. But
then he said, "Let's stay with the pass."

So the Eagles kept passing. And Johnny
Wolfe completed four of the next five throws,
moving the Eagles to the Bears' 30-yard line.

Then the passes stopped working. The
Eagles would have to try something else. In

the huddle, Johnny Wolfe looked at Rick. He said, "How about the number one trick?"

Rick thought about it. The number one trick was a play he and Johnny Wolfe had worked out together. Wolfe gave the ball to Rick. Rick made it look as if he were handing off the ball to another runner, but he really kept it. Then he dropped back and passed.

The play had worked well when the Eagles were working out. But they had yet to use it in a game. No one, other than Rick's teammates and coaches, knew that Rick could pass well.

No one but Mike, Rick thought. And then he was thinking about Mike again—about meeting him in a play-off game.

Wolfe touched Rick's arm. "Rick? Shall we bring out the trick?"

Rick came to and shook his head. "No. Let's save it. We may need it later."

"OK," Wolfe said. Then he called Rick's favorite running play.

In formation, Rick set himself. Then he rubbed his knees. He watched with sharp eyes as Wolfe took the ball from the center. Then, Wolfe dropped back, Rick crossed behind him and received the ball. With his legs moving fast, Rick started his swing around the left end.

It felt great to run. Holding the ball close, he moved down the field. Two yards. Five yards. Then he was hit. He went down.

Walking back to the huddle, Rick thought that he was finally on the move. Though short, the run had been his best of the game.

Suddenly, he saw someone get up from the bench and run onto the field. It was the man who took Rick's place when Rick wasn't playing. When the man came on the field, Rick had to leave.

Back on the bench, Rick felt sick and surprised. He felt more surprised when the coach came over and said, "That was a good run, Rick. That was the way you should *always* run."

"But I got stopped pretty fast," Rick said. "And you took me out."

"I'll tell you why." The coach sat down beside Rick. "There's a problem. Harry called down."

Harry was the Eagles' backfield coach. During every game, he sat high above the field and watched the play. If he saw a weak spot in the other team's game, he called it down by telephone to the Eagles' head coach on the field. If he saw that one of his own team's players was doing something wrong, he called that down too.

"What did Harry say?" Rick asked.

"Well, Rick, on that last play you rubbed your knees before you ran."

"Oh, not that again," Rick said. His old problem had come back. It was something he had tried to stop doing. In high school, he had made some small moves before running plays. He didn't know why he made them. Or even *that* he made them. But before running around left end, he would rub his knees. Before a run up the middle, he rubbed his nose.

Silly things. But he had had to work hard to stop doing them because they told the team he was playing against what he was about to do. In high school, and later in college, Rick had tried hard to stop these giveaway moves. This year, playing pro ball, his coaches had helped him more. For the most part, he had stopped making the moves. But the other teams knew about the moves. And he had just made one of them.

"I took you out because of that giveaway move, Rick," the coach told him. "You looked good on that last run, though. Real good. But try not to tell the Bears when you're going to make another run around the left end."

"OK," Rick said. "I'll watch it. I won't do it again."

The coach smiled and pointed at the field. "Then get out there, Rick. Get out there and get some points."

Rick ran onto the field. He was in the game again. And he knew he was ready to play well. But Johnny Wolfe called two plays in which Rick didn't carry the ball before he called Rick's favorite.

As blocks were made to clear the way for Rick's run, Rick took the ball and speeded around the left end. He had remembered not to rub his knees before the play began. So none of the Bears knew how he would run the play. Several of the Bears pounded down the field to tackle him. But Rick kept in front of them. A player threw himself at Rick from the side and caught Rick's arm. Rick started to fall. But he found his feet again and kept on running. The man was left behind on the grass.

Rick ran and ran. First right. Then left. Men kept coming at him. He pushed them off or moved out of their way. Once he had to spin all the way around to get free. But he did not go down.

Finally there was no one left ahead of him and no one fast enough to catch him. Rick raced over the goal line to the shouts of the people in the stands. With a wide smile, he threw the football high in the air.

After the extra point was kicked and made, the coach walked over to Rick. He said, "You know something, Rick?"

Rick looked up at him as he drank a cup of water. "What?"

"We're going to win this game."

And they did. Running again and again, and not giving away his plays, Rick piled up record yardage. And he made two more touchdowns. The Eagles won 28–7.

As the fans moved slowly out of the stands talking about the game, Howard Cosell added a few more words for the fans at home.

What Rick Huggard did during the second half I cannot believe! It was a new man out on that field. What turned Rick Huggard around? It must have been something deep inside him. . . .

Cosell went on, but Mike Huggard reached forward and turned off the television set. He looked at Dan Becker and said, "*Now* do you think he's not as good as I am?"

Dan shook his head. "I don't believe the yardage he picked up in the second half. And that footwork." He shook his head again. "It would be something, all right."

Mike made a face. "What would?"

"To see you and Rick playing against each other," Dan said.

"It won't happen," Mike said. "Our teams won't be playing each other this year."

"I think they will, Mike. I think it will be the Vikings against the Eagles in the first play-off game," Dan told him.

"No," Mike said. But even as he said it, he knew Dan was right.

CHAPTER 6

Heading for the Play-Off

Rick woke up in a room that looked over the city of San Francisco. Shaking his head to clear the sleep away, he walked to the window. Outside, the trees were blowing in the wind. It looked bright, but cold. Rick could see people on the streets below wearing heavy coats.

San Francisco. A game with the 49ers. If the Eagles won it, they would win their division title. And that would mean they would be in the first play-off.

A picture of Mike jumped into Rick's mind. If Mike's team won today too, they would win their division title. Then Rick and Mike would meet in the play-off.

Rick put the picture out of his mind. He didn't want to think about it. He wanted to think only about playing today's game.

A few hours later, Rick and his teammates boarded the bus for the stadium. Soon they were there. Everyone headed for the locker room. Not much later, they were ready to play. No one talked much. They all knew it was an important game.

When the Eagles ran out onto the field, only a few shouts could be heard from the crowd. But that didn't worry Rick. The Eagles were not the home team. Rick and his teammates would play their best, even if the crowd wanted the 49ers to win.

The Eagles won the coin toss. Rick sat on the bench and watched the 49ers' player kick the ball far down the field. The Eagles' receiver carried the ball up to the 20-yard line before he was brought down. Then Rick went in to play.

In the huddle, Johnny Wolfe called Rick's favorite play. Rick took his place and set himself. Then, as he waited for the ball, he rubbed his knees. He didn't know he was doing it. He was thinking only about the coming play. The Eagles' coach shook his head.

The play started as Johnny Wolfe took the ball from the center. In a second Rick crossed behind him and received the ball. With his head low and his feet racing, Rick started his swing around the left end.

As Rick ran, his blockers took out the 49ers defensive players one by one. Rick saw them fall to the ground as he moved across and up the field. With his great speed and his team's blocking, none of the 49ers got close enough to pull him down.

Soon there was only one player left who could stop him. Rick went right, then left as

the player came toward him. He wheeled right again. The player moved left. Rick sailed past him and down to the goal line. He scored. He had gone 80 yards on his first run.

Happy with himself, Rick ran slowly back to the bench. His teammates ran toward him, calling his name and hitting his hand with theirs. On the side of the field, the coach met him with a smile. "A great run, Rick," he said. "You had me a little worried, though. You rubbed your knees before the play. But it didn't matter. They still couldn't stop you."

When the extra point was made, the Eagles were ahead 7–0. Then the 49ers received, but after only three plays they lost the ball. Rick was sent onto the field.

In the huddle, Johnny Wolfe spoke. "We need to get a strong lead fast. We're going for the long pass."

Rick got set behind the line. He kept his hands from making any giveaway moves as Wolfe gave the call. Then, as Rick was moving to the side, he saw Wolfe take the ball from the center and drop back to look for his receiver.

Rick blocked his man as Wolfe let go a rocketing pass. It flew far down the field. But as it came down, a 49er caught the ball. He raced with it toward the Eagles' goal. With great speed, Rick was able to tackle him on the 20-yard line. But minutes later, the 49ers scored. With the score tied, Wolfe stopped throwing the ball and changed back to a running game. He called a lot of plays for Rick. And Rick ran them. He scored. But so did the 49ers.

Halftime came and went. In the second half, each team scored again. Rick began to tire. But he knew that he must keep playing his best.

Finally, less than a minute was left in the game. And the score was tied. The Eagles had the ball and were in a huddle.

Since Rick had been piling up yardage so well, Johnny Wolfe wanted to call a play for him. Rick had run 236 yards that day. The Eagles needed 44 more yards to score and win. Time was running out. Wolfe thought Rick was the right player to try for the score.

He looked at Rick. "Can you do it?"

"I don't know," Rick said. "The 49ers will be ready for me. Why don't we try the number one trick instead?"

Wolfe looked at Rick with surprise. "Will it work?"

"We'll make it work," Rick told him.

Rick was ready as he listened to Wolfe call the play. Then he ran left and took the ball from Wolfe's hands. Moving left again, he made it look as if he were handing off the ball to another running back, Jack Jenkins. But he didn't hand it off. He kept the ball instead.

Thinking that Jenkins had the football, the 49ers' line came after him. Jenkins led them off, giving Rick enough time to spot his receiver near the goal line. Rick pulled his arm back and threw. Then he watched the ball sail through the air.

At just the right time, the receiver turned and reached for the ball. He caught it. Touchdown! The Eagles had won.

The crowd in the stands didn't make much noise. For them, the wrong team had won the game. They were sorry to see the 49ers lose.

But Rick's team went wild. They jumped up and down and shouted. They ran to the locker room, laughing and pounding each other on the back. They had won the division title.

In the Eagles' locker room, television cameras and reporters were all over the place. The coach and many of the players were called on to talk. But Rick was the star. Everyone said so. Rick had never felt so good.

It was only after he had dressed and some of the noise had died down that Rick began to think about his brother again. The Vikings were playing for their division title today too. Was the game over? Had they won?

Rick walked over to his coach, who was still talking to a newspaper reporter. Calling him away, Rick asked, "Have you heard about the Vikings' game yet? Did they win?"

"They did, Rick," the coach said.

Suddenly Rick felt strange. With a blank look on his face, he said, "Then we'll be meeting them in the play-off."

* * *

All the way back to Philadelphia, Rick could think of nothing but the coming play-off game, when he and Mike would meet on the football field. As the big plane landed, most of Rick's teammates talked about going out on the town. But all Rick wanted to do was to go home and think some more. He wanted to ready himself for playing against Mike, to decide how he was going to handle it. When he reached home, he sat down without turning on the lights. His mind raced. What was he going to do?

As he sat worrying, the telephone rang. Rick picked it up. His father was on the line.

"You played a great game, Rick," Mr. Huggard said. "I saw you on television. It was one of your best games ever, and I wanted to call you up to tell you."

"Thanks, Pop," Rick said. Hearing his father's voice made Rick feel much better. Like Mike, Rick had been very close to his father since their mother had died. Rick had always tried to do well for him. And hearing his father's good words made Rick happy. "It means a lot to me to hear you say that," Rick went on.

"You earned it, Rick," his father said. "You earned a lot of people's good words today."

Rick smiled. It was good to be talking to his father again. Then the smile left his face. "Pop," he said. "Did you know Mike's team won too?"

"Yes," his father said, his voice suddenly soft. "His game wasn't on television like yours. But I did hear that the Vikings won."

"We'll be playing against each other, Pop," Rick said.

Rick's father didn't say anything right away. Then he said, "I know that too. It's something I never thought would happen. Something I hoped would never happen." The line was still again. Then Rick's father went on. "Do you remember when I talked to you boys a long time ago? About never playing hard against each other, about helping instead of hurting each other?"

"I remember, Pop," Rick said.

"You were only boys then," Rick's father went on. "You're men now. But what I said then I still believe. Brothers should love one another. I'm sorry to know you'll be fighting each other for a title."

Rick didn't say anything. He felt bad again. He asked his father, "Have you talked about this with Mike yet?"

"No," Mr. Huggard said. "But I will."

"Let me call him first, Pop," Rick said. "All of a sudden I want to talk to him."

"Go ahead, Rick," his father said. "And remember that I love you both."

After saying good-bye, Rick hung up the telephone. Then he put in a call to Mike.

It had been months since Mike and Rick had talked—since before the football season had started. Mike's voice sounded like it always did, like it did when Mike and Rick were boys together years ago. But when Mike knew that it was Rick who was calling, his voice changed. He sounded strange and stiff when he said, "How are you, Rick?"

"Fine," Rick answered. "I just talked to Pop. And talking to him made me want to talk to you. About—"

"There's nothing to talk about." The strange voice cut Rick off.

"But we'll be meeting in the play-off, Mike," Rick said. "We have to—"

Mike broke in again. "I know that, Rick," he said. "And I have nothing to say. I'll see you there."

With a soft noise, the telephone line went dead. Mike had hung up. Sitting back in his chair, Rick wondered about how cold Mike had sounded. But Mike had been right, Rick knew. There really had been nothing to say.

CHAPTER 7

Mountain Man Meets the Rookie

It was the day of the play-off. Since the Vikings and the Eagles had won the same number of games, there had been a coin toss to see in which hometown the game would be played. The Eagles had won the toss. On this clear, cold day, the Philadelphia stadium was filled with fans.

Inside the locker room, Rick sat on a bench. He was wearing his uniform. In minutes he would join his teammates and head for the field. But right now he was trying to square away his thoughts about the game.

He kept remembering the sports stories he had read all last week. They had been about Rick Huggard meeting Mike Huggard on the playing field. Younger brother against older brother. The rookie against the Mountain Man.

As Rick sat thinking, he felt what seemed like a hard knot inside. The knot had been there all week as he read and thought, and read and thought. Finally he had spoken to his coach about those stories. The coach had said they were just a way to build interest in the game. He had told Rick to forget about the stories and to think about playing well.

Rick had tried. But he had not been able to forget what he had read. Now, as he sat there, he knew he would have to forget about it. He had to face up to the game that was about to start. He would have to make himself play better than he had ever played before.

Seconds later, the coach called everyone together for a last talk. Then he said, "Let's go!"

Rick left the locker room with his teammates. Out on the field a band was playing. Cheerleaders were lined up. Flags were waving. As the Eagles ran across the field to their side, the crowd in the stands gave them a wild welcome. Rick felt ready to play the best game of his life.

The Vikings won the coin toss. They would receive. Rick sat on the bench as the Eagles' kicker sent the ball flying down the field. Then he watched as the Vikings' offensive team began working their way up the field.

For a few seconds, Rick took his eyes off the play. He looked over at the Vikings' bench. Since Mike was a defensive linebacker, he was sitting on the bench too.

Rick looked hard at him. Even across the field Mike looked like a giant. A giant made of stone—tough, never giving. But the giant sat

looking down at the ground. Rick had to fight against the hard knot he felt inside.

He pulled his eyes away. He made himself watch the game instead of his brother. He watched as the Vikings moved the ball. They missed the first down. When the kick came, the Eagles picked up the ball and moved it to their own 20-yard line.

The Eagles' offensive team headed for the field, and Rick went with them. He tried not to watch as his brother came onto the field too.

In the huddle, Johnny Wolfe looked at Rick. "Are you ready?" Wolfe asked.

"I'm ready," Rick said.

"Good," Wolfe told him. "Because they're waiting for you."

They, Rick thought. You mean *him*—my brother Mike. He thought about Mike's cold voice. Then he said, "I'll be glad to meet them."

Wolfe smiled, then called Rick's best play.

In formation, Rick set himself. Without knowing it, he rubbed his knees with his hands. Then he looked across the line. Mike was looking back at him. His face was hard, his eyes dark. Mountain Man, Rick thought. Just look at him.

Then Wolfe started calling the play. Rick took a breath as the quarterback took the ball from the center. Moving left, Rick crossed behind him, grabbed the ball, and started the swing around left end. The Vikings' end linebacker—not Mike—tried to pull him over. But Rick danced away from him, making it look easy.

Rick ran fast. He ran as well as he ever had. He felt happy. He was going to get past every tackle. He was going to run 80 yards again! Then he was hit from the side. He was hit so hard that he made a deep sound as he went down. Everything went black for a minute. His arms and side hurt as they had never hurt before.

When he could see again, Rick looked over to find out who had sent him crashing. Mike had just finished getting up and was moving back to his teammates. Of course, Rick thought. Who else could it have been?

Pushing himself up, Rick walked slowly back to his own huddle. No one said a word. Then Wolfe spoke to him. "Do we still have a ball game?"

Rick nodded. "We do," he said.

CHAPTER 8

The Longest 50 Yards

The first half of the game went by fast. At the end of the half, the Eagles were behind by two touchdowns.

Rick sat in the locker room. He looked at the floor, as he rubbed his hurting body. Mike had hit him hard—again and again. No matter which way Rick had run, Mike had been waiting for him.

With Rick being stopped, Johnny Wolfe had gone to passes. But they had been good for only one touchdown. The Eagles were feeling low. It seemed as if they had no hope of winning the game.

Before the second half was to begin, the coach called everyone together. He said,

"Keep playing hard, men. All of you are doing your best. I can't ask for more than that." Then he stopped for a minute.

Mike is doing his best too, thought Rick. He was playing like a man of iron. A man, not a boy. Not the way he and Rick used to play. He wasn't giving any ground. And he was jumping all over Rick.

The coach spoke again. "You're all playing hard. It's just that they're playing hard too. It's just that—"

"Rick's getting stopped," another player finished the coach's sentence.

Rick looked up.

"It's not Rick's fault," the coach said. "But—"

"It's true," Rick said. "I'm getting stopped." He wiped a hand across his face. "And look who's doing it."

* * *

The second half seemed a lot like the first. Rick was trying as hard as he could. But Mike dogged his every step. And the giveaway moves that Rick made every now and then helped Mike know what play Rick would be running. With his coach's help, Rick stopped himself from making them. And he started to make better yardage.

Things picked up for the Eagles. Johnny Wolfe started completing more passes. The Eagles were catching up. Near the end of the last quarter, they were only 4 points behind.

With time left for only two more plays, the Eagles stood on the Vikings' 35-yard line. The next few minutes would tell the story.

Rick stood in the huddle. His body hurt all over. Johnny Wolfe looked over at him. "We've got to move. How about the number one trick?"

"Let's give it a try," Rick said.

In formation, Rick waited for the play to begin. He held his hands still. Out of the corner of his eye, he saw Johnny Wolfe take the ball from the center. Racing left, he moved close to Wolfe as the quarterback handed off the ball to him. Then he made it look as if he were handing the ball to Jack Jenkins. But instead, he kept it.

The Vikings' line took off after Jenkins— everyone but Mike Huggard, Mountain Man. Mike came straight through and hit Rick as he stood looking for his receiver. He knocked

Rick for a 15-yard loss. The Eagles were now on the 50-yard line—50 yards away from the touchdown they needed to win the game.

The Eagles called time out. In the huddle, the quarterback looked around at his teammates. "There's no way we can make 50 yards in one play. Those 50 yards might as well be 1,000," he said. Wolfe had given up.

But Rick had not. He could not. He thought of those 50 yards. He thought of how he had run that many yards in one play before. He had made even longer runs on many other plays. And he wanted to make a long run now.

Wolfe took a deep breath. Then he looked at Rick. "OK," he said. "Let's give it a try. You've got the best hope of making it, Rick. Swing around left end?"

Rick didn't say anything for a second. Then he said, "My brother knows every move I'm going to make. He should. He's watched me play ever since we were kids. I want to make the run. But I can't get those 50 yards."

Wolfe shook his head. "Then what do you think we should try?"

Everyone looked at Rick. They wanted him to come up with the right answer.

"We can start like we did on the last play," Rick said. "You hand off to me, Johnny. Then, when Jack goes by me, I won't fake the hand-off to him. I'll *really* give him the ball. The Vikings will think we're using the number one trick again. They'll think I'm going to pass. So they won't go after Jack, they'll go after me. Maybe Mike will too."

Wolfe looked at Rick. "That play isn't even in our book," he said.

Rick knew that was true. But he knew it was the play that they needed. "It's in the book now," he said. Then he looked at Jack Jenkins. "Ready to run 50 yards, Jack?"

Jack Jenkins was another rookie—not as good as Rick, but still a team player. His eyes were bright now. "Yes," he said to Rick.

"That's it, then," Wolfe said. "Let's get out there and win."

Breathing fast, Wolfe called the play. As bodies met, he took the ball from the center. Then he handed it to Rick as Rick ran behind him. In a very quick move, Rick gave the ball to Jack Jenkins. Rick made it look as if he still had the ball.

Dropping back, Rick saw the Vikings' line running at him. Mike was in front. As Mike reached him, Rick lifted his hands, showing that he didn't have the ball.

Mike stopped short, surprised not to see the ball in Rick's arms. He stopped so fast that he fell. But he got up in a second and took off after Jack Jenkins. He pounded down the field. But Jenkins was far away. No one was near him as he raced across the goal line.

The people in the stands went wild. The Eagles jumped up and down and hugged each other. It was all over. The Eagles had won.

CHAPTER 9

Playing to Win

As the gun that ended the game sounded, Rick couldn't believe it was all over. They had done it. He called to Jack Jenkins and shouted in a happy voice with Johnny Wolfe.

Then, out of the corner of his eye, he saw Mike running toward him. There were people everywhere. But Mike made his way through. In seconds Mike was standing next to Rick, his arm around Rick's neck. He was smiling.

Rick couldn't speak. Where had the cold Mountain Man gone?

"Come on, rookie," Mike said to him. "These people will jump all over you. You're going to need some blocking. Come on, now. I'll clear a way for you to the locker room."

Still not believing it, Rick started to follow his big brother across the field. People called to him and tried to grab him. But Mike stayed in front of him, moving them out of the way.

Finally they were in the tunnel that led to the locker room. None of the fans could get in. Mike and Rick were by themselves for a minute. They looked at each other. Mike was smiling.

"When a football player gets to be a star, people want to touch him, get to him," he said. "You'll have to remember that from now on."

"You were the star today, Mike," Rick told him. "You stopped me on almost every play I ran. It was Jenkins who made that last touchdown."

Mike looked at Rick. "But who called for that play, little brother? Not the quarterback, I bet."

"Well. . ." Rick said.

"You did," Mike told him.

"You knew every move I was going to make. So I had to."

"You're growing up, Rick," Mike said, smiling again.

Now Rick smiled too. "It took me a while," he said. "You were always a star to me. You always helped me. And I never thought that I would be able to play in a game against you."

"I know," said Mike. "It was hard for me too. You're my little brother. Pop always told us to take care of each other, not to hurt each other. He was right. But we're older now. And we both have jobs to do. Playing pro ball isn't playing to hurt the other guy. It's playing the best way you know how. Playing to win."

"I think I know that now," said Rick. "And if we ever have to play each other again, we'll both be able to do it."

"Right," said Mike. "And the Vikings will get you the next time around."

"We'll see," said Rick, his arm around his brother's neck.

"Right now let's see about getting you into that locker room," Mike said. "I see a lot of reporters waiting to talk your ear off."